False Graining

TECHNIQUES

How to Add the Rich Look of Wood to Your Next Project

JIM KING & BETH OBERHOLTZER

FOX CHAPEL
PUBLISHING

"Call on your creative side and have fun with it! Don't stress if everything isn't perfect. Imperfections are part of the charm when you decorate by hand."

ABOUT THE AUTHORS

JIM KING is a "fancy painter" from Lancaster, Pennsylvania. He leads popular decorative painting and painted-box workshops and exhibits his work at traditional crafts shows.

Fascinated by the decorative painting on antiques he collected, Jim began studying grain painting in the 1980s. He purchased antique blanket chests at auctions and flea markets, restored them, and applied painted glaze surfaces. His research and experimention with color and technique allowed Jim to enjoy the exuberance of the craft and connect with his cultural past.

After Old Order Mennonite cabinetmakers copy his antiques in smaller sizes, he paints them using traditional techniques such as decorative motifs and grain painting.

Jim received his art degree from Goshen College in Indiana. In the 1990s he lived in Bangladesh, working for Mennonite Central Committee as a product designer. He is employed as the director of visual presentation and store design for Ten Thousand Villages, based in Ephrata, PA.

BETH OBERHOLTZER is a graphic designer, photographer, and writer from Lancaster, Pennsylvania. She grew up in a farmhouse where the grain-painted trim in the dining room and parlor was carefully preserved.

ISBN 978-1-56523-797-1

To learn more about the other great books from Fox Chapel Publishing, or to find a retailer near you, call toll-free 800-457-9112 or visit us at *www.FoxChapelPublishing.com*.

Note to Authors: We are always looking for talented authors to write new books. Please send a brief letter describing your idea to Acquisition Editor, 1970 Broad Street, East Petersburg, PA 17520.

Printed in China
First printing

Contents

Sample 1: **Graining Comb: Angled Technique 7**

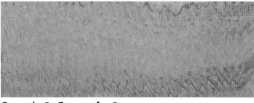

Sample 2: **Corncob 8**

Sample 3: **Graining Comb: Wavy Technique 9**

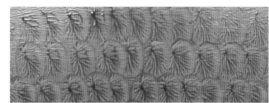

Sample 4: **Fingers & Hand 10**

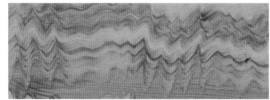

Sample 5: **Torn Cardboard 11**

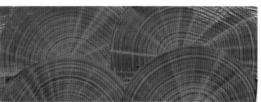

Sample 6: **Foam Brush 12**

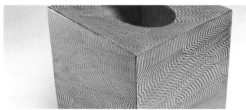

Project 1: **Tissue Box 14**

Project 2: **Mirror Frame 16**

Project 3: **Serving Tray 18**

Project 4: **Miniature Blanket Chest 20**

Project 5: **Block Frame 24**

Project 6: **Two-Drawer Chest 28**

Introduction

THIS hand-grained 19th century blanket chest is from the collection of author Jim King.

HISTORY

Grain painting is a type of decorative painting that imitates the grain in wood. Widespread among the American colonists and beyond in the 18th and 19th centuries, graining with paint offered an econcomical way to visually transform modest materials, such as pine, poplar, and maple, to simulate expensive hardwoods.

In a period when perserverance and hard work wove the fabric of life, this technical craft became an artistic outlet. What began as simple imitation evolved into a delightful representation of the artist's individuality.

Because homemade paints and tools were used to create finishes, the results were as varied as the painters. Many of the effects were merely suggestive of wood grain, often simply yielding an appealing repeat pattern.

As living conditions became easier, folk art designs varied more broadly. Some no longer mimicked the grained pattern of real woods but become wild designs.

NOTE: Acrylic- and oil-based transluscent glazes are used on the projects in this book. Early crafters often worked with a glaze made with vinegar for similar results.

GETTING STARTED

Using a decorative-painting technique called combing or graining, you can transform the plain surface of a utilitarian object into a textured and stylized veneer.

This method involves applying a dark, transluscent glaze over a yellow- or salmon-colored base coat and pulling a tool through the glaze while still wet to reveal the base coat. The result is a streaked finish that may resemble the grain of natural wood.

In this book, you will learn the basics. The tools and materials you'll need for the six projects are listed on page 5.

The Techniques section, beginning on page 6, shows the painting techniques you'll use to decorate each object.

There are step-by-step instructions for six projects beginning on page 13. The first three projects employ mass-produced, unpainted wooden items available at many craft stores. The next three projects employ handmade wooden chests and a block frame.

The base paint on the first five projects is golden yellow while the glaze is burnt sienna. Though the items themselves are different, the common colors allow you to compare the technique results more easily.

The final project, a two-drawer chest, is painted salmon pink, then a dark brown oil-based glaze is applied.

We suggest you read the techniques section before beginning any of the projects. That way you'll have a base of knowledge upon which to call when working through the project steps.

The final section of the book is a gallery showing a variety of finished pieces. For each is a list of the paint and glaze colors, and the tools and techniques.

Tools and Materials

TOOLS

- fine-grit sand paper
- 100% cotton cloths
- several 2" (5cm) foam paint brushes
- 2" (5cm) bristle paint brush
- small plastic cups to mix glaze
- graining comb
- corncobs
- lightweight chipboard (such as the backing from a small tablet)

To distress or antique

- sandpaper
- utility knife
- block of wood
- ring of keys

MATERIALS

- wood item for finishing
- acrylic latex paint for backgrounds (golden yellow, salmon pink)
- acrylic latex paint for trim (black, dark maroon)
- translucent color glaze (burnt sienna, brown)
- thinned amber shellac, made of one part amber shellac and one part denatured alcohol
- brown paste wax

SAFETY

While the materials listed here are not inherently dangerous, it's important to follow the manufacturers recommendations when using the paints, glazes, and shellac. If you have a skin sensitivity, wear gloves to avoid irritation. Wear a mask while sanding to keep from breathing in the dust. Work in a well-ventilated area.

NOTE: Some glazes are meant to be applied straight from the container. Others have manufacturers instructions on how to mix paint into the glaze and the suggested glaze-to-paint ratio. Experiment with different ratios to get the level of transparency that works best for your project.

Technique Practice

PREPARATION

Tools and Materials

- illustration board cut in 6" (15cm) panels
- 2" (5cm) bristle brush
- golden yellow and salmon pink base paint

1 Cut white illustration board into 6" (15cm) panels. A standard 20" x 30" (51 x 76cm) board will yield five sample boards. Prepare additional panels as needed.

In preparation for the projects in this book, it's a good idea to practice on illustration board. The next six pages suggest ways that you can explore creating visual textures in glaze using a variety of tools. Please consider the samples shown as simply starting points. No need to follow exactly what you see. Think about how the tools and medium speak to you. Your boards can serve as samples for reference. Feel free to practice at any time.

When you gain confidence after manipulating the glaze on sample boards, you'll be ready to move on to the projects beginning on page 13.

2 Paint each sample board with background paint and allow to dry overnight.

NOTE: In the 18th and 19th centuries, itinerant decorative painters carried painted boards to show samples of techniques they offered to customers. This was a precursor to today's decorator showrooms.

3 Assemble the tools you wish to use on your sample boards.

Graining Comb
Angled Technique

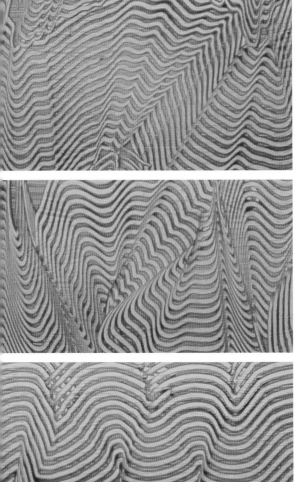

Paint one or two 3" (7.5cm) strips of glaze on your sample board with a foam brush. Leave a space between strips. Experiment with your combing tool on those strips, then paint two more strips. That way the glaze doesn't dry before you're ready to manipulate it.

Drag your comb through the glaze. Experiment with angle and degree of wave depth.

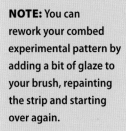

This is your opportunity to play! Use as many boards as you wish. It could be helpful to save them for reference as you individualize your technique.

SAMPLE 1

Drag a graining comb in small, undulating waves while changing direction to achieve an arresting variety of effects.

Comb painting technique used on project on page 14.

Tools and Materials
- prepared sample board
- 2" (5cm) foam brush
- burnt sienna glaze
- rubber graining comb

NOTE: You can rework your combed experimental pattern by adding a bit of glaze to your brush, repainting the strip and starting over again.

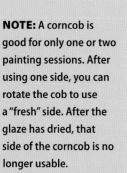

Corncob

SAMPLE 2

Drag a corncob through glaze for subtle variations in tone and texture. The cob here once held popcorn!

Corncob painting technique demonstrated on page 16.

Tools and Materials

- prepared sample board
- 2" (5cm) foam brush
- dried corncob
- burnt sienna glaze

NOTE: A corncob is good for only one or two painting sessions. After using one side, you can rotate the cob to use a "fresh" side. After the glaze has dried, that side of the corncob is no longer usable.

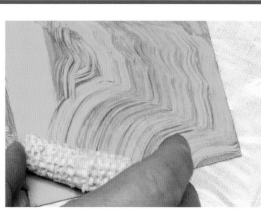

Paint a strip or two of glaze on your sample board with a foam brush. Experiment with different textures as you drag the corncob through the glaze. Change the angle abruptly or subtly.

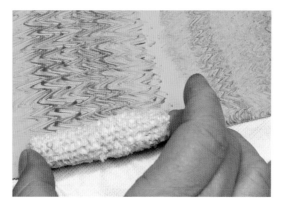

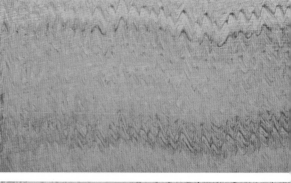

Try shifting the corncob up and down in a regular pattern as you drag it through the glaze. Vary the openness of pattern and the pressure of the corncob in the glaze.

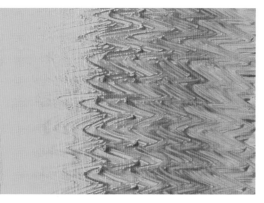

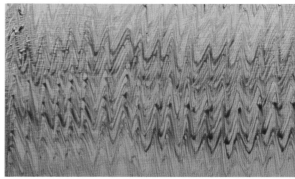

Break the cob in half and try a row of quarter- or half-circles to form a series of arcs.

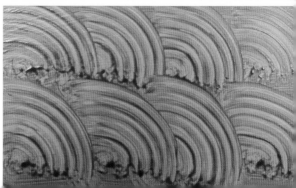

Graining Comb
Wavy Technique

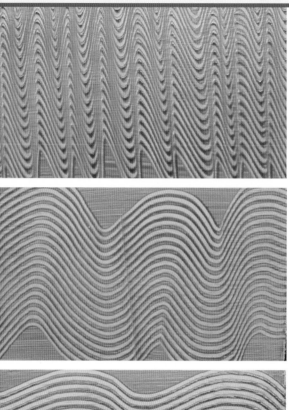

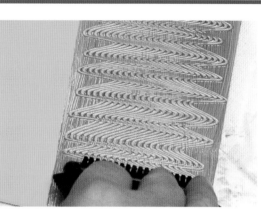

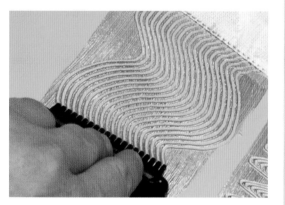

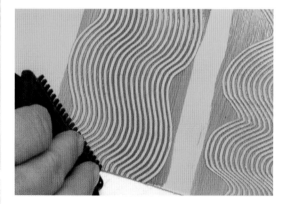

Paint a strip or two of glaze on your sample board with a foam brush. Experiment by dragging the comb through the glaze and shifting it up and down in a tight, regular pattern.

This time, drag the comb in a more open wave. Vary the amount of pressure to see how it affects the look.

Try a broad wave, then a very tight wave. Or, as shown at the bottom left, comb the glaze in one direction, then give the board a quarter turn and comb the glaze at right angles over top of the first texture. Some of your first combing will still be visible for a crisscross look.

SAMPLE 3

Again, drag your graining comb through the glaze. This time, keep the direction consistent and simply vary the depth of your waves.

Comb painting technique used on project on page 18.

Tools and Materials
- prepared sample board
- 2" (5cm) foam brush
- rubber combing tool
- burnt sienna glaze

NOTE: Shown here is a rubber graining comb. There are many other combs on the market made out of different materials and in a variety of shapes and sizes.

False Graining Techniques

Fingers & Hand

SAMPLE 4

Fingerpainting is not just for children. Glaze manipulation with fingers and hands is fun and quirky.

Finger painting technique used on project on page 20.

Tools and Materials

- prepared sample board
- 2" (5cm) foam brush
- dark brown glaze or burnt sienna glaze

NOTE: Try moving the side of your hand through the glaze, as illustrated at the bottom right.

Dabbing with the tip of your finger makes a delightful star-shaped pattern.

The side of your hand produces a varied vertical pattern.

Touching down with the pad of your finger results in a starburst within an oval.

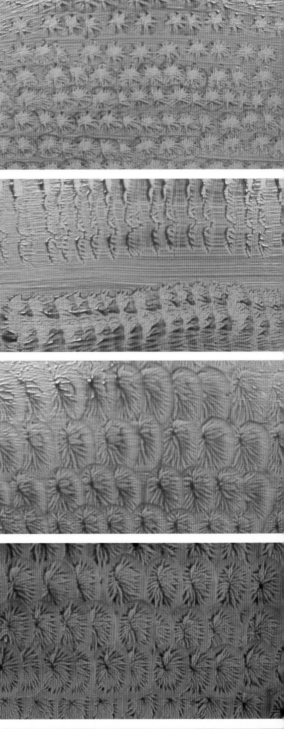

Torn Cardboard

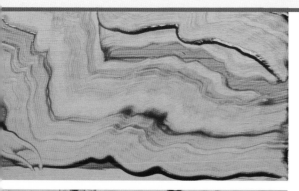

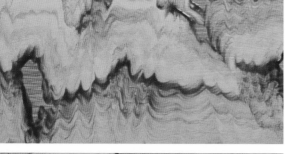

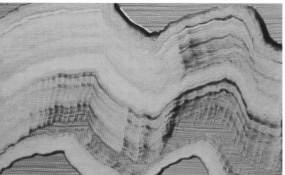

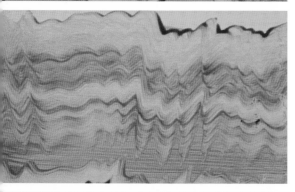

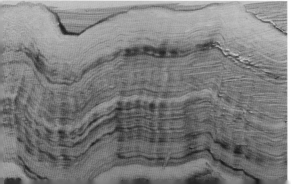

Paint a strip or two of glaze on your sample board with a foam brush. Experiment by dragging your torn cardboard through the glaze. Try angling it down, at a diagonal, then across.

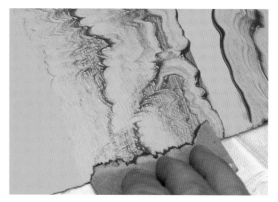

Add a shimmy and a twist as you create a freeform burnt sienna landscape.

Or drag the cardboard through the glaze while applying subtle sideways wiggles and changes in pressure.

SAMPLE 5

The irregular edge of torn cardboard can yield dramatic contrasts as it dips and turns through the glaze.

Torn cardboard painting technique used on project on page 24.

Tools and Materials
- prepared sample board
- 2" (5cm) foam brush
- piece of lightweight chipboard (such as that from the back of a tablet)
- burnt sienna glaze

NOTE: A piece of torn cardboard is good for only one painting session. After the glaze has dried, the cardboard is no longer usable.

False Graining Techniques

Foam Brush

SAMPLE 6

The humble foam brush shows its impressive versatility as you dab, swipe, and swirl it through the glaze.

Foam brush painting technique used on project on page 28.

Tools and Materials
- prepared sample board
- 2" (5cm) foam brush
- brown glaze

Paint a strip or two of glaze on your sample board with a foam brush. Use the same foam brush to experiment with textures. Drag it across the glaze while executing a series of tight ups and downs.

Try dabbing the tip of the brush to form a row of vertical lines in the glaze. Repeat the row a half-step down, partially overlapping the first row.

NOTE: The dark brown glaze shown in use on this page is oil-based. When working with oil, remember that the room should be well ventilated and 24 hours of drying time is necessary.

Get dramatic results by rotating the brush in graceful half-circles. Begin at the top left, make a row to the right, then make a second row partially overlapping the first.

Projects

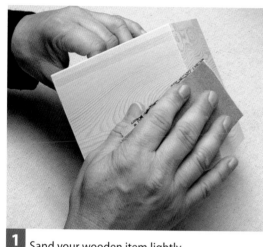

1 Sand your wooden item lightly.

The condition of your wooden item dictates the amount of preparation needed. Typically you'll need to sand the item, wipe the dust off, and apply two coats of base paint.

A smooth, clean surface allows better control and consistency as you apply and then manipulate the glaze.

If you decide to decorate a piece of furniture that has already been painted and varnished, you'll need to sand the entire surface. You may wish to visit thrift stores or flea markets for items that you could revive by repainting and decorating.

Tools and Materials

- wood item for finishing
- fine-grit sand paper
- 100% cotton cloths
- 2" (5cm) bristle brush
- golden yellow or salmon pink base paint

2 Make sure you sand the openings and all edges.

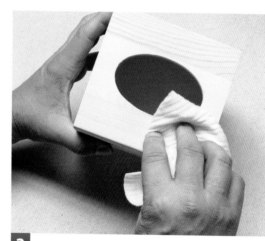

3 Wipe the dust off with a soft cotton cloth.

SEQUENCE FOR EACH PROJECT

Preparation

1. sand
2. wipe off dust
3. paint base (two coats)

Manipulation

4. paint glaze
5. manipulate glaze with tool

Finishing

6. shellac glazed sections
7. paint dark details (if applicable)
8. shellac whole piece a second time

Distress if you choose

1. create wear and tear effect
2. sand
3. wax

4 Paint the item with a coat of base paint using a 2" (5cm) bristle brush. No need to drench it. You'll be applying a second coat.

5 The second coat is especially important if you are working with a mass-produced item. The paint will help fill irregularities in the wood.

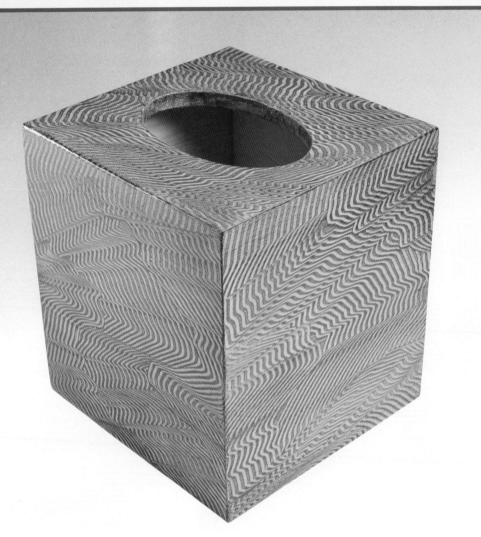

Tissue Box

PROJECT 1

This painted facial tissue box is the perfect mix of utilitarian and decorative!

Manipulation technique explored on page 7.

Tools and Materials

- unfinished wooden tissue box
- rubber graining comb
- 2" (5cm) bristle brush and 2" (5cm) foam brush
- fine-grit sandpaper
- golden yellow paint
- burnt sienna glaze
- thinned amber shellac

1 Sand the wooden box and wipe off the dust. Apply a coat of yellow paint and allow it to dry. Apply a second coat.

2 Using a foam brush, paint burnt sienna glaze on one side of the box. Make sure the glaze extends to all edges.

3 Drag the graining comb in a regular waving and twisting pattern through the glaze-painted section. Allow the side to dry for an hour.

4 Rotate the box a quarter turn and apply glaze. Immediately comb in a pattern similar to the first side.

NOTE: Use short vertical strokes when you glaze the inside edge of the hole. Do not comb that edge.

5 The first stroke on each side follows a meandering diagonal from the top left to the bottom right.

6 Fill in remaining sections in a similar wave pattern. Repeat combing on the other two sides of the box with an hour drying time between each.

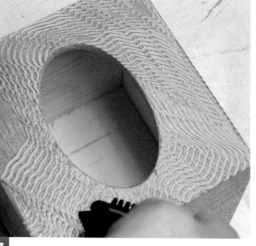

7 Apply glaze to the top of the box and comb it. Allow the box to dry overnight.

8 Finally, apply two coats of thinned amber shellac with two hours drying time between coats.

NOTE: It is possible for you to rework your design if you're unhappy with the combed results. If the glaze is still wet, simply add a bit more glaze to your foam brush, repaint the section and comb a new design. If you want to redo the design a few hours later after the glaze is dry, wipe the glaze off completely with a damp rag. Reapply glaze and comb a new design.

Mirror Frame

PROJECT 2

This plain frame becomes special with the delicate and varied corncob texture. Pop in the mirror and reflect on your skills!

Corncob painting technique explored on page 8.

Tools and Materials

- unfinished wooden frame
- dried corncob
- 2" (5cm) bristle brush and 2" (5cm) foam brush
- fine-grit sandpaper
- golden yellow base paint
- burnt sienna glaze
- thinned amber shellac

1 Sand the wooden frame and wipe off the dust. Apply a coat of yellow paint and allow it to dry. Apply a second coat.

2 Using a foam brush, apply yellow paint under the edge of the frame's opening. This is important because the inserted mirror reflects that edge.

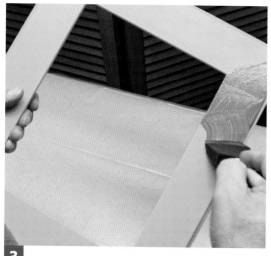

3 Paint burnt sienna glaze on the front side of the frame with a foam brush. Make sure the glaze extends to all edges.

4 Drag the corncob top to bottom in a regular waving pattern through the glaze-painted section on one side of the frame.

5 Rotate the frame counter-clockwise and manipulate the glaze in a downward motion on the second side. Rotate and do the third side.

6 Create a similar visual texture on all four sides. If you're displeased with a result, you may reapply glaze if necessary and drag the cob down again.

7 Make sure you match the beginning and final angle of your corncob with the mitered corners of the frame on each side. Allow to dry overnight.

8 Apply two coats of thinned amber shellac with two hours of drying time between. Your frame is now completed and ready to hold a mirror.

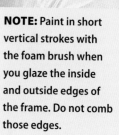

NOTE: Paint in short vertical strokes with the foam brush when you glaze the inside and outside edges of the frame. Do not comb those edges.

NOTE: The corncob used to manipulate the glaze on the frame at the left is from popcorn. Other kinds of corncobs work equally well. Experiment.

False Graining Techniques

Serving Tray

PROJECT 3

This decorated tray can corral your TV remote controls and cell phones in a unique and stylish way.

Comb painting technique explored on page 9.

Tools and Materials

- unfinished wooden tray
- rubber combing tool
- 2" (5cm) bristle brush and 2" (5cm) foam brush
- fine-grit sandpaper
- golden yellow base paint
- burnt sienna glaze
- thinned amber shellac
- black trim paint

1 Sand the wooden tray and wipe off the dust. Apply two coats of yellow paint on the sides and ends, allowing it to dry between coats. Do not paint the inside of the tray.

2 Using a foam brush, paint burnt sienna glaze on one side of the tray and on the top edge of that side. Do not glaze the inside of the tray.

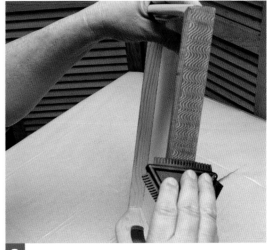

3 Drag the rubber combing tool in a tight waving pattern through the glaze-painted side section.

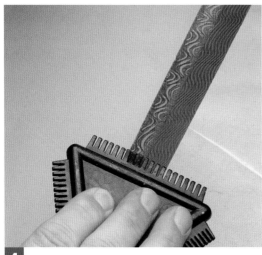

4 Immediately comb the narrow top of that side in a tight wave pattern also. Allow it to dry for an hour, then repeat on the other side of the tray.

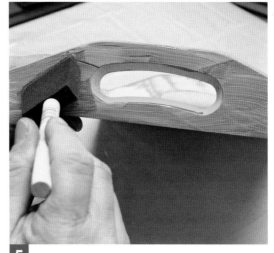

5 After the sides dry, paint the flat end of the tray and the top edge of the end with glaze.

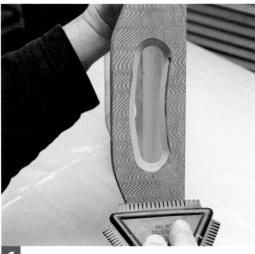

6 Drag the comb down in two vertical strokes, matching the tight wave look you achieved on the side panels. Comb the top of the end.

7 Allow to dry, then glaze and comb the other end. Apply a coat of thinned amber shellac only on the painted sections of the tray.

NOTE: Use short vertical strokes when you glaze the inside edges of the handles. Do not comb these edges.

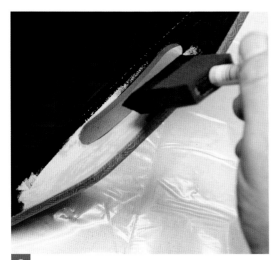

8 Paint the inside of the tray black. The shellac on the decorated sections will allow you to wipe off bits of black that go astray.

9 Add a second coat of black. After it dries, apply two coats of thinned amber shellac to the entire tray, inside and out. Allow it to dry between coats.

Miniature Blanket Chest

PROJECT 4

It's hard to picture anything more personalized than a piece carrying your fingerprints!

Finger painting technique explored on page 10.

Tools and Materials

- unfinished small chest
- 2" (5cm) bristle brush and 2" (5cm) foam brush
- fine-grit sandpaper
- golden yellow base paint
- burnt sienna glaze
- thinned amber shellac

Optional

- four small wooden finials
- wood glue

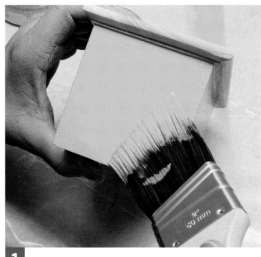

1 Sand the wooden box and wipe off the dust. Apply a coat of yellow paint and allow it to dry. Apply a second coat.

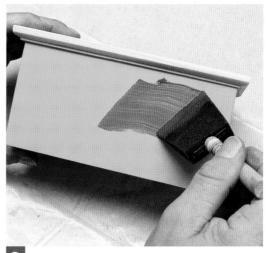

2 Using a foam brush, paint burnt sienna glaze on the front side of the box. Make sure the glaze extends to all edges.

3 Gently press your finger into the glaze, forming rows of prints. The box here is held upside-down without the lid.

4 Begin your first row along the straight edge and work your way down. That way you can easily see your previous row as you proceed.

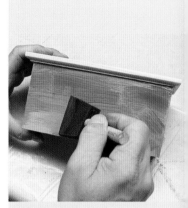

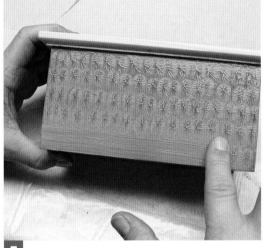

5 Your rows of finger prints should be regularly and evenly placed. Allow the side to dry for an hour.

6 Rotate the box a quarter turn, apply glaze, and repeat the finger print pattern. Allow the end to dry.

NOTE: After you initially paint each surface with glaze, stroke the foam brush through the glaze again. This provides a smooth surface for you to texturize.

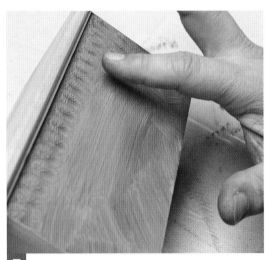

7 Rotate the box and paint glaze onto the back side of the box and dab with your finger.

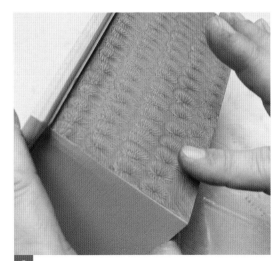

8 Make sure your fingerprint spacing matches what you've done on the other sides.

False Graining Techniques

MINIATURE BLANKET CHEST

NOTE: Early furniture painters typically used a narrow range of dark colors for trim. Dark green, black, and brick red are shown above, while the block frame on page 24 is accented with dark red.

9 Rotate the box and paint glaze on the end. Dab with your finger in multiple rows to match the established pattern.

11 Now it's time to dab your finger on the lid. Continue with the same spacing and rows that appear on the sides and ends.

13 Apply a coat of thinned amber shellac with a bristle brush to the decorated sections and allow it to dry.

10 Set the box aside and paint glaze on the lid. Make sure the glaze extends completely to the edges.

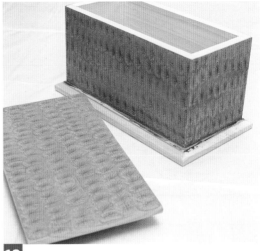

12 You can see here how the rows on the side and end of the box align. It can also work very nicely if you choose to dab in a more random fashion.

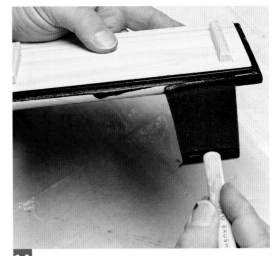

14 Switch to the foam brush to paint the edge of the lid and the trim at the bottom of the box black.

15 The shellac on the decorated sections will allow you to wipe off bits of black that creep onto the decorated sections.

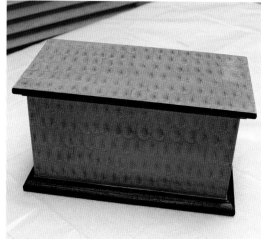

16 You may choose to apply the final coat of shellac at this point, or add feet as shown in the next photo.

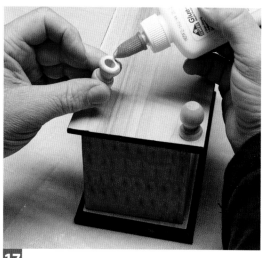

17 Using wood glue, attach the four round feet at the four corners on the bottom of the box. Allow to dry two hours.

18 Apply a second coat of black to the trim and feet. You may wish to use masking tape to ensure a clean edge. Let it dry overnight.

NOTE: In the eighteenth and nineteenth centuries, blanket chests often had round feet, called bun feet. You can create this look for your box by attaching wooden finials from your local craft store.

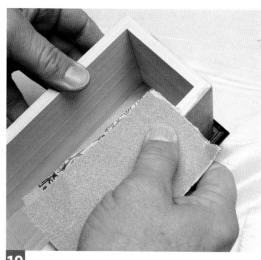

19 If bits of paint or glaze have found their way onto the top edge of the box, sand them off for a clean look.

20 Finally, apply a coat of thinned amber shellac to the entire outside of the box and lid.

Block Frame

PROJECT 5

Who would have guessed that torn cardboard can bring such dramatic results!

Torn cardboard painting technique explored on page 11.

Tools and Materials

- unfinished wooden frame
- piece of lightweight chipboard (such as the backing from a small tablet)
- 2" (5cm) bristle brush and 2" (5cm) foam brush
- fine-grit sandpaper
- golden yellow base paint
- burnt sienna glaze
- thinned amber shellac
- dark red trim paint

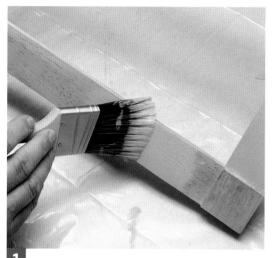

1 Sand the frame and wipe off the dust. Apply two coats of yellow paint, allowing it to dry between coats. Paint the sides only, not the corner blocks.

2 Select a piece of lightweight chipboard such as the backing from a small tablet. The cardboard should be a bit wider than the side of the frame.

NOTE: The rubber combing tool shown above helps imitate the look of malachite.

3 Tear the cardboard to form an irregular edge.

4 Using a foam brush, paint burnt sienna glaze on one side of the frame. Do not glaze the corner blocks or the outside edge.

5 Drag the torn edge of the cardboard through the glaze from the top block to the bottom block.

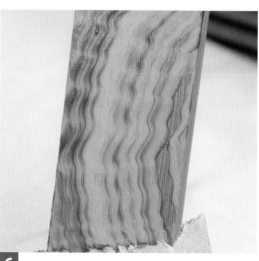

6 Use a waving movement as you draw the cardboard piece through the glaze.

NOTE: Crafters use a variety of tools to manipulate glaze. You might consider using natural or manufactured sponges, balled up tissue paper or newspaper, plastic wrap, leather strips, feathers, bristle brushes, potatoes, and more.

BLOCK FRAME

NOTE: As you gain experience, the materials and techniques in this book can be combined in a variety of ways. Your design will depend on the tools you choose, the manipulation you employ, and the colors of base paint and glaze. Simply follow the steps established and adjust as needed to suit your piece.

7 Make sure your design begins and ends against the corner blocks and that you don't leave gaps next to the blocks.

8 Use short vertical strokes when you glaze the inside edge of the frame. Do not comb that edge.

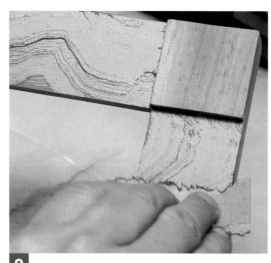

9 Rotate the frame a quarter turn. Apply glaze and draw the cardboard piece down the second side. Match the look of the first side you decorated.

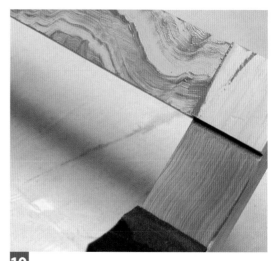

10 Rotate the frame a quarter turn and apply glaze on the third side.

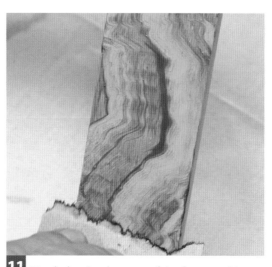

11 Match the visual texture of the first two sides as you drag the cardboard down the third side.

12 Note how the hills and valleys of the cardboard edge create the darks and lights of the pattern.

13 The cardboard piece deteriorates with use. You'll want to choose a small project when you decorate with this method.

14 Use the bristle brush to apply a coat of thinned amber shellac on the glazed portions of the frame.

NOTE: If your workshop has high humidity, the glaze may wander and blur the design, as shown above. Compare that to the clearly defined visual texture below.

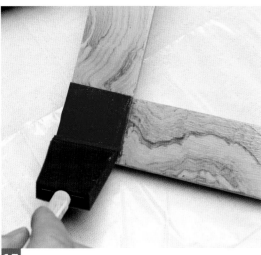

15 Paint the top and edges of each corner block dark red using the foam brush.

16 The shellac on the decorated sections will allow you to wipe off bits of dark red that creep onto the decorated sections.

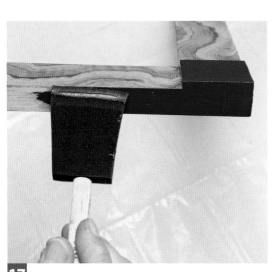

17 Paint the outside edges of the frame dark red, allow it to dry for two hours, and then paint all the trim a second time. Allow it to dry overnight.

18 Finally, apply two coats of thinned amber shellac with two hours of drying time between coats.

Two-Drawer Chest

PROJECT 6

The personality of this chest emerges after you apply paint and distress it to create the look of years of use.

Foam brush painting technique explored on page 12.

1 Sand the wooden box and wipe off the dust.

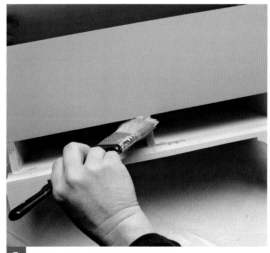

2 Apply two coats of salmon pink paint, allowing it to dry after each coat. You do not need to paint the sections that will be detailed in black.

3 Using a foam brush, paint brown glaze on the top of the box. The glaze should stop at the edges that will be detailed in black.

4 Using the same foam brush, draw the tip of the brush along the glaze while moving it up and down in a regular pattern.

5 Repeat the manipulation in a series of rows. Instead of leaving a gap, each row should overlap the previous row. Allow to dry overnight.

6 Turn the box and apply glaze to one end. Use smooth, straight brush strokes.

7 Again draw the tip of your foam brush through the glaze in undulating rows, maintaining your visual rhythm.

8 Overlap each row with the previous, ending neatly at the bottom edge. Allow the end to dry overnight, then repeat the process on the other end of the chest.

TWO-DRAWER CHEST

Tools and Materials

- unfinished box
- 2" (5cm) bristle brush and 2" (5cm) foam brush
- fine-grit sandpaper
- salmon pink base paint
- oil-based brown glaze
- thinned amber shellac
- paste wax

NOTE: Some prefer using oil-based rather than acrylic-based glaze because of the history of the technique and the visual depth it brings to the graining. These positives offset the possible negatives of strong fumes, longer drying times and more complicated clean-up.

False Graining Techniques

9 Turn the chest so that the front is face-up. Apply glaze in even strokes.

10 Draw the tip of your foam brush in undulating rows through the glaze, repeating your established pattern.

NOTE: Look for old wooden items at flea markets and thrift stores. Frames, boxes, trays, and chests can be given new life!

11 You can go back and redo a section that isn't to your liking if you work while the glaze is still wet.

12 Apply glaze to the front of one of the drawers and manipulate the glaze. Repeat on the second drawer front.

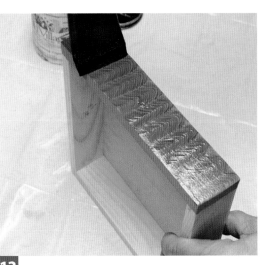

13 It is important to match the look of the front of the box when you manipulate the glaze on the drawers since they'll be viewed as one unit.

14 Since the front, top drawer edges are sometimes visible, make sure you paint them. Use short regular strokes when you apply the glaze.

15 After the glaze has dried, shellac the decorated sections of the chest. When that has dried, you're ready to paint the trim black.

16 Use a clean foam brush to paint the trim black. Depending on the steadiness of your hand you may wish to tape off sections to ensure a neat edge.

NOTE: Turn bright, new brass knobs into antiqued versions. Strip off the protective lacquer, then brush with vinegar and allow to dry. If you want the color darker, repeat the process. When satisfied with the patina, wash the vinegar off with water.

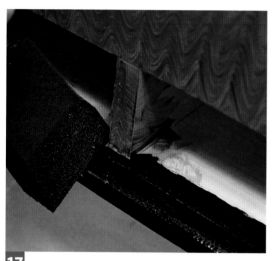

17 The black paint needs to extend beyond where the drawers rest to make sure there is no raw wood visible when the drawers are in place.

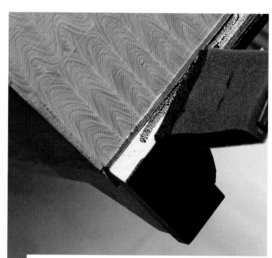

18 After your first coat of black trim has dried, apply a second coat. Allow that to dry.

19 Apply a coat of thinned amber shellac to all surfaces, inside and out.

20 After the shellac has dried, you may consider your box finished. Or go a step further and distress it as shown on the following two pages.

NOTE: Shellac, composed of natural resin, was the primary finish used by woodworkers in years past. Along with being historically accurate, the yellow cast in amber shellac adds a warm glow to your project's freshly painted surfaces. There are varieties of varnish that may also be suitable to finish your piece.

False Graining Techniques

Finishing

Tools and Materials

- thinned amber shellac
- 2" (5cm) bristle paint brush
- utility knife
- ring of keys
- wooden block
- fine-grit sand paper
- brown paste wax
- cotton cloth

SEQUENCE FOR EACH PROJECT

Preparation

1. sand
2. wipe off dust
3. paint base (two coats)

Manipulation

4. paint glaze
5. manipulate glaze with tool

Finishing

6. shellac glazed sections
7. paint dark details (if applicable)
8. shellac whole piece a second time

Distress if you choose

1. create wear and tear effect
2. sand
3. wax

NOTE: To care for your completed box, simply dust it with a dry cloth.

SHELLACKING

1 Shellac your piece as a final step or just before distressing. In most cases it is not necessary to shellac the inside of your box or back of your frame.

2 A coat of shellac on unpainted surfaces, especially on larger pieces, can give an extra-finished look to your piece and will make warping less likely.

DISTRESSING

Creating the look of wear and tear is an effective way to add depth and dimension to a piece. Study antiques to identify wear patterns and how you can imitate authentic aging.

The two-drawer chest is the only project in this book that has been distressed; however, the techniques explained here can be applied to any of the other projects.

In addition to the tools shown, you might consider using a chain, hammer, screwdriver, or steel wool to give your piece an implied backstory.

Regulate the force of your aggression based on the sturdiness of your piece.

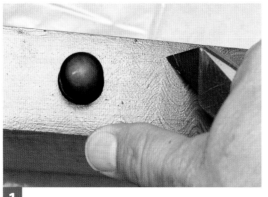

1 Use a utility knife to nick bits out of the surfaces. This exposes small patches of the base paint color or raw wood.

2 Slap a ring of keys against the flat surfaces in a random fashion to imitate the hard knocks life has dealt.

3 Strike all edges of the chest repeatedly with a wooden block.

4 As you distress the chest, pay special attention to parts that would have been subject to the most wear over the years.

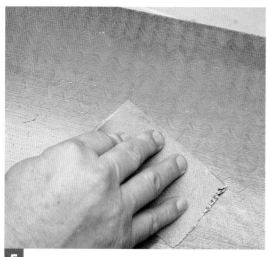

5 Sand the chest lightly. After sanding, do *not* wipe off the dust. The dust mixes with the wax that is applied next to contribute to the aging affect.

6 Sand down through painted sufaces in high wear areas, such as around drawer pulls and on edges and corners.

NOTE: The two photos above show one foot of the chest before it was distressed and the same foot after it was distressed. Notice how "aging and wear" have resulted in small nicks, worn edges, and a slightly dulled patina.

7 Rub a generous amount of wax into the entire painted surface of the chest with a soft cotton cloth.

8 This is an opportunity to be imprecise! Leave bits of paste wax in corners to suggest the build-up of years of grime.

False Graining Techniques

Idea Gallery

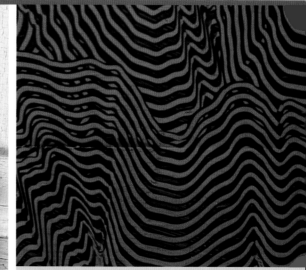

Country Queen Anne Frame

Base color: vermilion
Glaze color: oil-based black
Manipulation technique: graining comb
Trim color: black

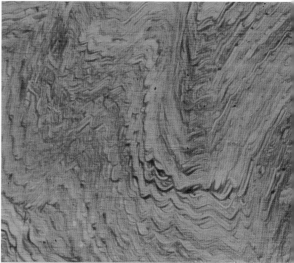

Antique Candle Box with New Surface

Lid base color: golden yellow
Glaze color: acrylic-based mocha
Manipulation technique: corncob
Box color: black

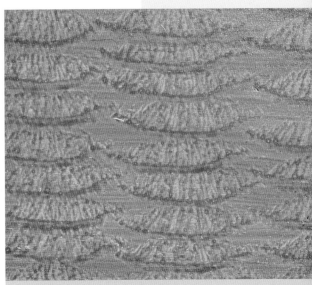

Two-Drawer Chest

Base color: golden yellow
Glaze color: oil-based brown
Manipulation technique: bristle fan brush
Trim color: black

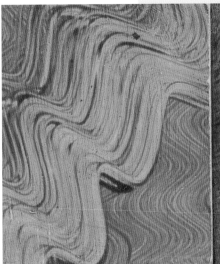

Block Corner Mirror Frame

Base color: golden yellow
Glaze color: acrylic-based mocha
Manipulation technique: corncob
Trim color: black

Ogee-Footed Storage Box

Base color: golden yellow
Glaze color: acrylic-based mocha
Manipulation technique: graining comb
Trim color: black

Bible Box

Base color: golden yellow
Glaze color: acrylic-based mocha
Manipulation technique: cut half of potato
Trim color: black

Stenciled Tool Box

Base color: golden yellow
Glaze color: acrylic-based mocha
Manipulation technique: foam brush

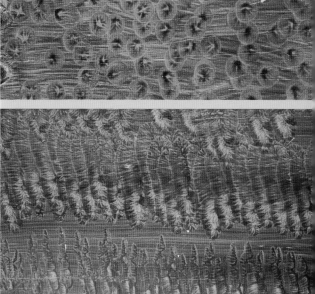

Antique Reproduction Candle Box

Base color: golden yellow
Glaze color: oil-based brown
Manipulation technique: fingers and hand

Round Box

Base color: golden yellow
Glaze color: acrylic-based burnt sienna
Manipulation technique: graining comb

Reproduction Sewing Box

Base color: golden yellow
Glaze color: acrylic-based burnt sienna
Manipulation technique: graining comb
Trim color: black

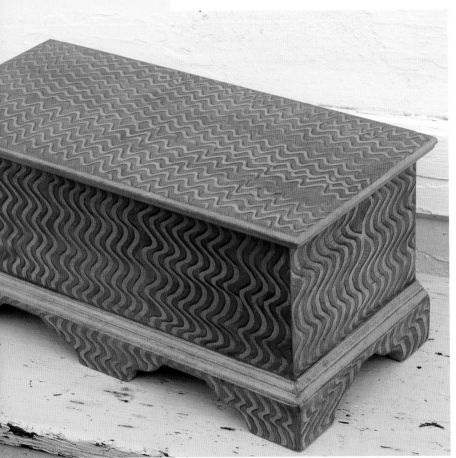

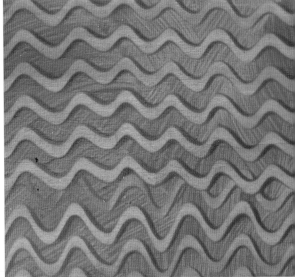

Jewelry Box

Base color: golden yellow
Glaze color: acrylic-based burnt sienna
Manipulation technique: plastic drywall applicator
Trim color: golden yellow

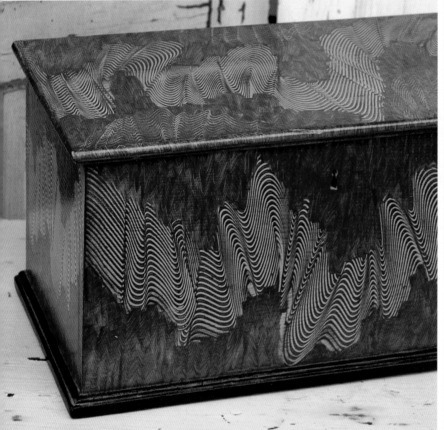

Document Box

Base color: golden yellow
Glaze color: acrylic-based mocha
Manipulation technique: foam brush, graining comb
Trim color: black

Flat Photo Frame

Base color: salmon pink
Glaze color: oil-based dark red
Manipulation technique: fingers

Bracket-Footed Mini Chest

Base color: golden yellow
Glaze color: acrylic-based mocha
Manipulation technique: malachite comb
Trim color: black

More Great Books from Fox Chapel Publishing

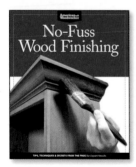

No-Fuss Wood Finishing
ISBN 978-1-56523-747-6 **$19.99**

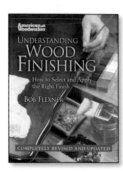

Understanding Wood Finishing
ISBN 978-1-56523-566-3 **$24.95**

Great Book of Shop Drawings for Craftsman Furniture, Revised Edition
ISBN 978-1-56523-812-1 **$29.99**

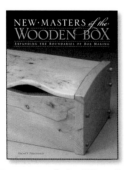

New Masters of the Wooden Box
ISBN 978-1-56523-392-8 **$29.95**

18th Century Furniture
ISBN 978-1-56523-608-0 **$19.95**

Woodworker's Guide to Veneering & Inlay
ISBN 978-1-56523-346-1 **$24.95**